School Conflict

Tish Davidson

Franklin Watts
A Division of Scholastic Inc.
New York • Toronto • London • Auckland • Sydney
Mexico City • New Delhi • Hong Kong
Danbury, Connecticut

Dedication

For my daughters, Helen and Susan

Cover illustration by Peter Cho.
Cover and interior design by Kathleen Santini.
Illustrations by Pat Rasch.

Library of Congress Cataloging-in-Publication Data

Davidson, Tish.
    School conflict / by Tish Davidson.
        p. cm. — (Life balance)
Summary: Explores the issues surrounding aggression and violence in schools, looking at the origins and history of school violence, as well as contemporary methods of preventing and dealing with the problem.
Includes bibliographical references and index.
    ISBN 0-531-12251-4 (lib. bdg.)   0-531-15571-4 (pbk.)
    1. School violence—United States—Juvenile literature. 2. Conflict management—United States—Juvenile literature. [1. School violence. 2. Violence. 3. Conflict management.] I. Title. II. Series.
    LB3013.32.D39 2003
    371.7'82—dc21

                                        2003000106

Table of Contents

School Conflict, Past and Present

When Heather McCutcheon's family moved just before she started the fifth grade, everything fell apart. Although Heather had once been well liked and had enjoyed school, she now felt awkward and out of place. Suddenly her clothes weren't right, her hair wasn't right, and she couldn't seem to say anything right.

Things only got worse. "In the locker room one day, I saw a group of girls breaking into the locker of a girl I knew. They were throwing her things in the garbage and reading her journal. When I asked them what they were doing, they sneered and told me to

5

mind my own business." As Heather was leaving, a teacher stopped and asked her what was going on in the locker room. "I stuttered; I stammered. How could I lie? So I told her the truth."

Tattling was considered the most heinous crime in school, and word got around. Within a week, Heather couldn't walk home without a group of girls taunting her. "We're gonna kick your butt. You're dead meat! You little snitch, you think you're smart?" One day, three girls surrounded her. For twenty minutes, they called her names, put her down, and spit at her. "If you move, we'll kick your butt," they threatened. When the girls finally let her go, Heather ran home in tears.

For the next two years, this experience affected every aspect of Heather's life. "I would eat and eat, just to look busy. I would find quiet little places at school, so no one would find me. No one cared. No one ever took the time to find out why I was crying in the bathroom. No one

"I would eat and eat, just to look busy. I would find quiet little places at school, so no one would find me. No one cared."

asked me why I had so many sick days, or why I spent so much time in the nurse's room, hiding under the blanket with a mysterious stomach pain."

Violent Teachers

Today, most school conflicts occur among students, but this has not always been the case. Until the mid-1800s, children were not required to go to school, so children whose families could afford it educated them with tutors at home. For these privileged children, school conflict did not exist. In 1852, Massachusetts became the first state to pass a law requiring that all children attend school until they are sixteen years old. Other states soon passed similar laws, as did Canada and Great Britain. New students poured into unprepared schools. Teachers with no experience in managing large classes were expected to educate rowdy children, many of them teens who had never been to school before. During this time, a teacher wrote in his journal that, in one year, his class had driven out four other teachers before he was hired. The students had thrown one teacher out the door and tossed another out the window.

To maintain order in their classrooms, teachers turned to corporal punishment. In the 1850s, corporal punishment—hitting, smacking, spanking, beating, and flogging—was considered an acceptable way for adults to control children. Although local school boards sometimes discouraged corporal punishment, it was common for teachers to discipline students by hitting. Despite exceptions (New Jersey, for example, banned corporal punishment in schools in 1867), the practice remained legal in twenty-three states even as late as 2002.

The Education of Winston Churchill

Until the middle of the twentieth century, beating students was a common and accepted form of discipline in schools in the United States, Canada, and Great Britain. British statesman and Nobel Prize winner Winston Churchill attended St. George's School in 1882, when he was eight years old. He wrote in his autobiography, My Early Life, *"Two or three times a month the whole school was marshaled in the Library, and one or more delinquents were hauled off to an adjoining apartment by the two head boys, and there flogged until they bled freely, while the rest sat quaking, listening to their screams... How I hated this school, and what a life of anxiety I lived there for more than two years."*

Gradually, the idea that teachers should use physical force to control students fell from favor. Between 1970 and 2000, half the states in the United States and many more individual school districts passed laws forbidding the use of corporal punishment in schools. This reduced the amount of violence occurring between students and teachers, but conflict among students gradually increased.

The Rise of Student Violence

Some pushing, stealing, taunting, and fighting has always occurred in schools. However, in the 1950s, violence at school—especially serious violence associated with gangs—became more common. From the 1950s through the 1970s, the number of crimes committed by young people at school increased significantly. Some school violence was associated with political causes, such as protests against school integration or against the Vietnam War. In addition, society was changing. Increased use of illegal drugs, greater family instability due to divorce, the popularity of graphic movies and violent song lyrics, and easy access to guns contributed to the increase in violence. By 1978, young people were twice as likely to be victims of crime at school than anywhere else.

In response, schools put more emphasis on campus security. They hired guards and installed metal detectors and surveillance cameras. School officials made regular locker inspections or eliminated lockers altogether in an attempt to keep weapons and drugs out of schools. Some schools even had police officers assigned to them.

It worked. The trend of increased school violence was reversed. By 1998, students were only half as likely to be victims of a serious crime at school as they were outside school. But a frightening thing happened. Although the number of incidents of school conflict decreased, the late 1990s brought a new and more lethal kind of violence: A few alienated students brought guns to school and shot teachers and other students, often at random.

School Shootings: A New Generation of Violence

In the past, serious school violence was usually limited to fistfights and knife fights. These fights generally involved only a few students, and the conflict was often diffused before anyone was seriously hurt. Once guns appeared on school campuses, everyone became a potential target. Students and teachers could be ambushed or shot at from a distance. Gunshot wounds were often disabling or fatal. Angry shooters did not seem to care who they shot, concerned only that they hurt large numbers of people.

Although the chances of being involved in a school shooting were small, the unpredictability of these attacks made students and teachers believe that they were more vulnerable than before. Suddenly, schools did not feel like safe places anymore, as school administrators, mental-health professionals, and law-enforcement officers were being asked to explain violent events that, on the surface, seemed inexplicable.

How Violent Are Our Schools?

The national media coverage of school shootings, especially the rampage that occurred at Columbine High School in Colorado, made it seem as if schools were more unsafe than at any time in the past. However, in the 1998 school year, only sixty violent deaths occurred at schools in the United States: forty-seven murders, twelve suicides, and one person shot by a police officer in the line of duty. Of the sixty deaths, forty-two of them (about 70 percent) were students. Although it seemed that school violence was a new, dramatically increasing, out-of-control problem, a comparison of indicators of school conflict from 1990 to 2000 shows that overall, the level of serious school violence has remained steady or has even declined.

Changes in School Violence between 1990 and 2000

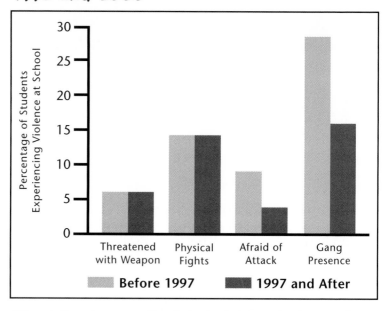

Although there is a perception that school violence has increased, conflict on middle-school and high-school campuses remained the same or decreased between 1990 and 2000. (Source: United States Department of Education, National Center for Education Statistics, 2000.)

Today, fewer than 1 percent of murders and suicides of school-age children happen at school. Still, many students worry about school shootings and aggression in other forms, as they cope every day with an environment of low-level conflict—pushing, shoving, taunts, and threats—while trying to get an education. Our schools, which are supposed to provide a safe place to learn and grow, are hostile places for many students.

Accident Prone?

A 1998 NBC/Wall Street Journal poll found that 71 percent of American adults thought it was likely that a school shooting could happen in their community. When the odds of dying in a school shooting are compared to the odds of dying in other types of accidents, it appears that this concern is exaggerated. For example, the chances of dying in a motor-vehicle accident are about 320 times greater than dying in a school shooting, yet students ride to school in buses and cars every day with little anxiety about their safety.

Type of Accident	Odds of Dying
Motor vehicle crash	1 in 5,900
Medical or surgical error	1 in 84,000
Falling on stairs	1 in 192,000
Airplane crash	1 in 382,000
School shooting	1 in 2,000,000
Lightning strike	1 in 4,300,000

(Source: Based on one-year odds from statistics collected and calculated in 1999 by the National Safety Council, the National Center for Health Statistics, and the United States Census Bureau.)

Two

Bullying and Harassment

Until he reached middle school, Jason had always enjoyed school. But by October of the seventh grade, he found himself hating school days. The problem was Alex, another seventh grader. "It started on the bus at the beginning of the year. Alex would make fun of my clothes, my backpack, even the way I walked. He kept calling me a sissy and asking if I was gay."

Jason tried to ignore Alex, but things got worse. Alex would trip him or push him whenever he got the chance. "If I was with one of my friends, he would yell 'Hey Jason, is that your boyfriend?' Pretty soon none of the guys wanted to be seen with me." In the crowded halls of Ridgeway Junior High, no teachers seemed to notice Alex's taunts.

Soon, every morning, Jason was waking up with a knot in his stomach, dreading the coming school day. One morning, he complained so much about feeling sick that his mother kept him home, and his stomachache went away. But the next morning, it was back. "I really did feel sick. I wasn't faking," remembers Jason.

Jason's reaction to Alex's bullying is not unusual. A 1996 study published in the *British Medical Journal* found that victims of bullying were three times more likely than other children to have problems sleeping, three times more likely to feel sad, and twice as likely to have regular headaches and stomachaches.

Victims of bullying were three times more likely than other children to have problems sleeping, three times more likely to feel sad, and twice as likely to have regular headaches and stomachaches.

As Alex stepped up his attacks, Jason's stomachaches got worse. After missing several days of school each week because of stomach pain and nausea, Jason's mother took him to the doctor for a checkup. The doctor found nothing physically wrong, but Jason's stomach complaints continued. Some mornings he even threw up. Eventually, the doctor suggested that Jason see a therapist.

Over time, the therapist helped Jason open up and talk about his anxieties and his problems with Alex. At the therapist's suggestion, Jason's mom began driving him to school, rather than having him take the bus. She made sure that school officials knew that he was being bullied, and she asked that Jason and Alex have no classes together. "Alex still bugged me sometimes, but I hardly ever had to see him," said Jason. "It was hard going back to school, but each day that I didn't have to deal with Alex, it got a little easier."

School conflict does more than cause physical harm. It also causes emotional distress and anxiety for the people who are involved and even for those who just see it happen. Even the threat of violence can make students change their habits and avoid certain places in school, such as bathrooms, where they feel unsafe. Fear of being teased, bullied, or harmed causes some students to skip classes or avoid going to school altogether. Even when students do go to school, the worry that they may be involved in conflict can interfere with their concentration, ability to learn, and their enthusiasm for school. Often parents and teachers are not even aware that a student feels threatened.

> ### Skipping School
>
> *Between 2 percent and 5 percent of American children are afraid to go to school. These students regularly develop physical symptoms such as headaches, upset stomachs, and dizziness when it is time to go to school, and they use the symptoms as a reason to stay home. Separation anxiety, worry about a situation at home, and lack of self-confidence often cause younger students to stay away from school. In middle school and high school, major causes of school avoidance include fear of bullies, stress from being teased, and anxiety about being involved in violence either at or on the way to or from school.*

Bullying and School Violence

Once school shootings focused attention on the problem of violence in schools, teachers, parents, and mental-health workers began to look more closely at daily low-level conflict in schools. "Most school conflict arises from gossip, name-calling, harassment, bullying, boyfriend/girlfriend issues, cliques, and in-groups," says Marcia Peterzell, an expert in school-conflict resolution from San Francisco, California.

Name-calling, says Peterzell, involves an occasional taunt. Harassment is a pattern of repeated name-calling and put-downs. Bullying is intentional repeated intimidation or aggression by a person with more power toward a person with less power. The power can be physical when one person is larger or stronger than another, or it can be emotional, as when one person humiliates another. Power imbalance also occurs when one person has a weapon and the other does not. Although not all bullying involves physical violence, the threat of harm underlies all bullying.

Bullying creates an environment of fear and hostility in a school. It is different from spur-of-the-moment aggression, because bullies plan their attacks and intentionally select targets who are weaker than themselves. Bullies do not empathize with their victims or feel guilt about their actions. They enjoy their power and prey on the same person over and over. Often bullies have high self-esteem because they feel that they are in control.

Both boys and girls can be bullies. Boys tend to use physical methods of bullying such as pushing, tripping, fighting, or stealing. Girl bullies are more likely to use verbal and emotional tactics such as excluding someone from the group, humiliating someone, and spreading gossip or false rumors.

No one is quite sure how many students in the United States are bullied. One study done at the University of Illinois found that, at the beginning of the school year, about one out of every four students was being bullied. By the end of the school year, the number had dropped to about one out of every thirteen students. The people who conducted this research suggest that bullies start the school year looking for people to intimidate. When they find a person whom they can hurt, they bully that person over and over and leave other students alone.

Bullies often do not think that they are doing anything wrong. They rarely see their behavior as hurtful, because they cannot empathize with or imagine the feelings of their victims. Perhaps you recognize some of these characteristics of a bully in someone you know. Bullies:

- feel they have to control every social situation
- put down people they dislike rather than avoid them
- think that being bigger or stronger makes them better or more important than others
- cannot stand to be wrong; they have to stand up for their opinions and prove that they are right in every situation
- believe that people who get in their way deserve the bad things that happen to them
- enjoy starting rumors or gossiping about people they dislike
- feel that to look good they must be the leader of their social group and control who is a member of the group
- have parents who encourage them not to let other people push them around

- feel that other kids are out to get them and that they must fight back
- make plans to get revenge on people they think have hurt them
- have often been exposed to models of aggressive behavior
- mistakenly interpret hostile intent in the actions of others
- are quick to anger and the first to use force

Bullying reaches a high point in middle school. About one in ten middle-school students say that they are bullied, while only one in fifty high-school students feel bullied. Some experts think that these numbers are too low, and probably twice as many students are actually being bullied. Some students may not report bullying because they are embarrassed to admit that they are a victim or because they do not define the aggression that they are experiencing as bullying.

Many adults downplay the harm that bullying does and consider it just part of growing up. Despite what the numbers say, the effects of bullying are widespread. Bullying affects everyone who sees it happen, not just the bully's target. In fact, some kinds of bullying, such as humiliation or exclusion, are effective only if there is an audience.

Assault... or Accident?

On the first day of school in 2001, Jeffrey Figueroa, a middle-school student in Walnut Creek, California, was waiting in line for a locker assignment. "I pulled out a gum wrapper and rolled it around my finger, and put a little point on it," Figueroa later told ABC News. "I asked my friend, 'How far do you think this can go?' And he said, 'I don't know,' and I blew it in the air."

The gum wrapper Jeffrey so casually launched ended up in the right eye of a fourteen-year-old classmate, Nicholas Trainer. The eye was injured, and Nicholas was taken to the hospital and later underwent eye surgery.

Jeffrey was suspended from school. Then, three months later, criminal charges were filed against him in connection with this incident. Jeffrey was charged with battery causing serious bodily injury, assault with a deadly weapon, assault by force likely to produce great bodily injury, and mayhem—all felonies that could bring years of jail time.

After a three-day trial in juvenile court, Jeffrey was found guilty of battery causing serious bodily injury and mayhem. The maximum sentence he could receive was eight years in juvenile prison. Instead, Judge Araceli Ramirez sentenced him to one week in juvenile detention, 150 hours of community service at an eye bank, and mandatory attendance for the family at anger-management and counseling sessions. She also set a 7 P.M. curfew as part of Jeffrey's home probation.

Many people questioned the severity of the sentence for what Jeffrey's mother called "a terrible accident" and his lawyer called "childhood behavior." However, the prosecution made the case that the spitball incident was part of an ongoing pattern of aggressive, bullying behavior. At the trial, about twenty neighbors testified that Jeffrey and his brother often ran wild in the neighborhood and that their behavior seemed threatening. During the sentencing, the judge criticized Jeffrey's parents for refusing to recognize and take steps to stop their sons' aggressive behavior.

On the other hand, Kimberly Trainer, the mother of the student who was injured, said that she thought the sentence was too light and did not make Jeffrey truly accountable for his actions. She claimed that Nicholas continued to suffer both physical and emotional trauma as a result of the incident. After the criminal case against Jeffrey was decided in October 2002, Trainer filed a separate civil court suit seeking financial compensation from the Figueroas.

Bullying can be mild or severe. Mild bullying includes activities such as shoving, casual put-downs, name-calling, and excluding someone from activities. Although almost everyone does these things occasionally, when these actions are aimed repeatedly at the same person, they become harassment or bullying.

Moderate bullying includes spreading hurtful rumors, intimidation, threats, punching, tripping, and intentionally damaging another's property. Severe bullying crosses the line into serious school violence. Severe bullying includes kicking or fighting to cause injury, threatening with weapons, demanding money or property (extortion), stealing, and destroying another person's possessions.

In addition to causing physical injury, bullying can cause extreme emotional distress. Teen suicides in North America, Europe, and Asia have been linked to severe school bullying. In November 2000, Dawn-Marie Wesley, a fourteen-year-old Canadian, hung herself in her basement. She had been repeatedly pushed, teased, and threatened by three older girls at her school to the point where she feared for her life and was afraid to walk home alone. She left a suicide note saying, "If I try to get help, it will get worse."

To Dawn-Marie, it seemed as if committing suicide was the only way to stop the threats and abuse. Meanwhile, she hid her pain from the outside world. Until her death, her family had no clue that she was having trouble with bullies.

In a landmark case, the three girls who had threatened Dawn-Marie were charged with criminal harassment. Two of the girls were found guilty, while the third was acquitted, or declared not guilty. The guilty teens received sentences of probation and community service.

Bullycide

"Bullycide" is a British word used to describe a suicide that is caused by bullying, teasing, or harassment. British experts believe that thousands of children attempt suicide each year because they are bullied at school and that at least sixteen children die every year from bullycide in Great Britain.

Other Kinds of School Aggression

Other aggressive behaviors that increase the hostile environment at schools are sexual harassment and hate threats. Verbal sexual harassment involves unwanted and inappropriate comments about another student's body, sexual activities, or sexual preferences. Physical sexual harassment includes inappropriately touching, pinching, or caressing someone who does not want to be touched.

Hate threats involve the use of hate-related words or symbols directed at people because they belong to a particular group. Hate-related words create hostile stereotypes. They target people because of their race, ethnic background, religion, gender, sexual orientation, or disability. According to the United States Department of Justice, 13 percent of middle-school and high-school students say

Who Hears Hate Words?

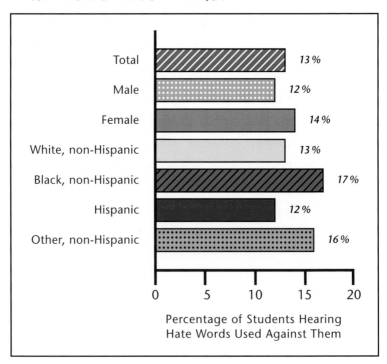

Percentage of Students Hearing
Hate Words Used Against Them

Hate words are used against people who are deemed different from those around them. No ethnic or racial group is exempt from feeling the sting of hate. (Source: United States Departments of Education and Justice, October 2000.)

that they regularly hear hate words used against them at school. More than one-third of these students also say they have seen hate-related graffiti at school.

Many of the students who carried out school shootings during the 1990s seem to have felt bullied, harassed, and excluded from mainstream school life. But bullying alone is not enough to explain why some students "snap" and bring guns or bombs to school. Most people who feel bullied or isolated at school never become violent. They never bring weapons to school nor turn them on their tormentors or themselves. Although aggressive bullying behavior and school violence overlap, there is no undisputed proof that bullying is the direct cause of school violence. To understand more about why some students become violent at school, we must look at other factors in their lives and the role violence plays in our society.

The Making of
a School Shooter

April 20, 1999, began as any other Tuesday at Columbine High School in Littleton, Colorado. Until almost lunchtime, teachers and students went about the ordinary high-school business of teaching and learning. Suddenly, at about 11:20 A.M., shots rang out. Explosions followed, then chaos. As students ran screaming from the school, they saw two gunmen in ski masks, armed with assault weapons, firing at them.

A teacher made one of the first emergency 911 calls. "I'm a teacher at Columbine High School, and there is a student here with a gun. The school is in a panic, and I'm in the library. I've got students down," she is heard telling the dispatcher, on tapes later released by the police. What followed was the worst school shooting in American history.

> ## "I'm a teacher at Columbine High School, and there is a student here with a gun... I've got students down."

When the gunfire stopped, twelve students and one teacher were dead and more than twenty other people were wounded, some seriously. The gunmen, eighteen-year-old Eric Harris and seventeen-year-old Dylan Klebold, both students at the school, then turned the guns on themselves and committed suicide.

After searching the school and the boys' homes, police found four guns and more than thirty home-made bombs. Eric wrote in his diary that he and Dylan had hoped to kill at least 250 people during their attack on the school. The nation was shocked at the attack on Columbine High School. When information the gunmen left behind showed that the destruction had been carefully planned for more than a year, people began to ask how parents, teachers, and friends could have missed the signs that Eric and Dylan were angry and potentially violent.

Who Becomes Violent?

After Columbine, people could see that they had ignored warning signs that Eric Harris and Dylan Klebold were troubled young men. However, there is no specific checklist of behaviors to show that they would become school shooters. On the surface, Eric and Dylan appeared to be little different from many other high-school seniors. The son of a retired Air Force officer, Eric was academically talented and described by some as charismatic. He lived in a stable, middle-class, two-parent home. Dylan seemed even less likely to become violent. He went to his school's prom, played fantasy baseball, and had been accepted at the University of Arizona. He also came from a stable family.

However, both boys had been in minor trouble with the law. They were arrested for breaking into a car, and a classmate had complained that Eric had threatened to kill him. For a while, Eric maintained a hate-filled website containing information on how to make bombs. Although his website promoted destruction, it was allowed to remain online because it contained no specific threats against individuals. Still, no one would guess that Dylan and Eric would leave five homemade videotapes outlining their hatred of their schoolmates, their plans for revenge, and their desire to be famous.

The Worst School Massacre in the United States

School massacres are not new. Although the gunfire at Columbine High School caused the most shooting deaths on a school campus, even worse school violence occurred on May 18, 1927, in Bath, Michigan. On that day, school-board member Andrew Kehoe planted dynamite in the basement of the Bath Consolidated School. When the dynamite exploded, it killed thirty-nine students and teachers; dozens more were injured. Kehoe then committed suicide by blowing up himself and four other people using more dynamite. Kehoe was angry about paying higher school taxes when he did not have enough money to make his mortgage payments and was going to lose his farm. In 1992, the state of Michigan erected a historical marker in Bath in remembrance of the tragedy.

Warning Signs

After the events at Columbine High School and several copycat school shootings that followed, the United States Secret Service was asked to make recommendations on how to prevent school violence. Its report, released in October 2000, concluded, "There is no accurate or useful profile of a school shooter."

If there is no accurate way to determine which young people will become violent at school, how can parents, teachers, friends, and mental-health workers know who needs help and when to get involved? No one set of features fits all violent students. However, mental-health professionals, physicians, and law-enforcement officers have developed a list of behaviors and characteristics that increase the likelihood of a person behaving violently. These characteristics are *only* guidelines. Many of the warning signs are common to any person who is dealing with problems or going through an emotionally difficult time.

Warning signs for violent behavior show up in three areas: home life, school life, and personal behavior. Problems at home often carry over into problems at school. Students who come from dysfunctional families—families unable to cope well with the stresses of daily life—are more likely to try to solve their problems with violence than those who come from families with better problem-solving and coping skills. Middle-school and high-school students recognize that home problems often carry over into conflict and violence at school. In an Alfred University study conducted in 2001, 61 percent of students said they believe that being physically abused at home is a cause of school violence; 54 percent said that simply seeing violence at home is a reason people become violent at school.

Factors That Increase the Risk a Student

Home-life factors

School-life factors

Personal-behavior factors

Will Become Violent :

- Being physically abused
- Witnessing domestic violence
- Having a parent abusing alcohol or drugs
- Having a parent with mental illness
- Experiencing extreme family stress

- Being bullied
- Feeling humiliated or disrespected
- Feeling isolated or excluded
- Earning poor grades
- Lacking interest in school or community activities
- Feeling disconnected from adults

- Displaying an inability to control anger
- Abusing alcohol or drugs
- Carrying a weapon
- Belonging to a gang
- Deriving pleasure from hurting people or animals
- Participating in vandalism
- Lacking problem-solving and communication skills
- Being mentally ill

Feeling Shut Out

For most teens, school is the center of their social lives. When students feel humiliated, bullied, isolated, or friendless, school can become a difficult and hated place. Some students respond by dropping out or enrolling in alternative schools. Others hide their humiliation as best they can and keep silent. Many become depressed. A few reach the point where they hate school and their schoolmates so much that they turn to violence.

Bang Bang You're Dead

William Mastrosimone wrote a play explaining how school stress, jealousy, and conflict can escalate into violence and killing. The play, Bang Bang You're Dead, *is available free of charge for performances by schools and youth groups. It also served as the basis for a Showtime movie of the same name. For more information about* Bang Bang You're Dead, *go to www.bangbangyouredead.com.*

Many of the school shooters in the late 1990s felt isolated, picked on, and friendless. Elizabeth Bush of Williamsport, Pennsylvania, one of the few girls to become a school shooter, allegedly wounded another girl in the cafeteria because Elizabeth had been teased and threatened repeatedly. Eric Harris and Dylan Klebold both left diaries with comments about how they had been mistreated by their fellow students.

As a survey by Alfred University researchers indicates, students recognize the stress of being an outcast at school. Although students said that experiencing violence at home is a significant reason why students become violent at school, almost 90 percent said the main reasons why school shootings occur include having other kids pick on, make fun of, or bully students at school and these students getting revenge on those who had hurt them.

Personal behavior also influences how likely someone is to become involved in school violence. Because drug and alcohol use decreases self-control, angry situations can turn into ugly conflicts more quickly when drugs and alcohol are involved. Carrying a weapon increases the chance that the weapon will be used. Gang membership increases peer pressure to use force instead of reason to solve problems.

The presence of a few warning signs does not mean that a person will automatically become violent. It does suggest, however, that a person feeling troubled, unhappy, and angry might benefit from professional counseling or talking to a trusted adult. The more of these risk factors that are present in someone's life, the greater the chance that he or she is severely troubled and will turn to violence. If someone you know shows many of these warning signs, encourage that person to talk about his or her feelings to a mature, caring person.

Are You Depressed?

Everyone has bad days when they feel tired and discouraged. Although people occasionally say they are depressed—meaning down in the dumps—depression is actually a clinical term that describes unexplained sadness lasting for weeks or months. Depression is thought to be caused at least in part by a chemical imbalance in the brain that affects the transmission of nerve impulses. Sometimes it is triggered by a specific event, but most often depression comes on gradually for no obvious reason.

One in every twelve teenagers experiences depression. The following are some questions to help you determine if you might be depressed. If you answer yes to three or more of these questions, you should seriously consider talking to an adult about how you are feeling.

For more than two weeks:

- have you felt sad and unhappy?
- have you had trouble sleeping?
- have your eating habits changed?
- have you felt restless and irritable?
- have you had trouble concentrating?
- have you stopped enjoying activities that you used to enjoy?
- have you felt like a failure?
- have you felt guilty for no particular reason?
- have you felt as if you are not as good as other people?
- have you cried often or felt like crying?

Depression should not be ignored. Although depression assessment tests do not diagnose depression, they do show whether you are at risk for depression and if you should seek help about the way you are feeling. With the help of a professional, depression can be treated successfully with psychotherapy (talk therapy) and medication.

Turning the Pain Inward

Some young people, instead of taking their anger out on others, turn their anger and pain inward. Some cut their bodies. Others threaten, attempt, or commit suicide. Although only a tiny percentage of suicides occur at school, teen suicide is a major problem. It is the third leading cause of death (after motor-vehicle accidents and homicide) among people ages fifteen to twenty-four. In 1999, about one in every five high-school students said that they had considered suicide.

No one knows why some students hurt themselves or others while the vast majority does neither. Depression is thought to play a role in both suicide and homicide, but again, most people who are depressed do not become violent. Some mental-health professionals see both suicide and homicide as responses to hopelessness and the feeling that there is no alternative except destruction. Others believe suicide and homicide are both expressions of anger and rage.

Suicide is a preventable tragedy. The following are some of the warning signs that a person may be thinking of attempting suicide. These changes in behavior are only guidelines, and not everyone who demonstrates them is at risk for suicide. However, these behaviors often indicate that a person is under extreme emotional stress and would benefit from talking to a mental-health professional or trusted adult:

- talk of hopelessness

- talk or threats about suicide or an excessive interest in death and dying
- sudden withdrawal from friends and activities; a preference for being alone
- changes in sleeping, eating, or socializing patterns
- decreased interest in school, work, or friends
- talk about feeling guilty or worthless
- impulsive, dangerous, aggressive behavior, such as driving recklessly, drug or alcohol abuse, or risky sexual activity
- unexplained generosity or the giving away of possessions
- talk of not being around in the future or the saying of good-byes

If you see some of these warning signs in yourself or in a friend, seek adult help. Don't assume that adults will not understand or will not believe how you feel. Most adults, in fact, vividly recall the ups and downs of being a teen. Heather McCutcheon remembers how it felt: "I'm out of high school, but I still carry the pain from junior high, when I was told that I was nothing and would never be good enough to belong. But now I have compassion for the bullies out there. They missed out on a really great friend—me— because someone had taught them that the only way to make themselves feel good inside was to put others down."

Four

Society's Role in School Violence

The way students respond to stress, anger, disappointment, or frustration depends on their personal experiences, family values, coping skills, and the emotional support available to them. But students are also influenced by the culture in which they live. It is difficult, however, to separate which cultural factors are important and which uniquely personal characteristics contribute to the way in which students handle situations leading to school conflict. This is one reason why no one can accurately predict which students will become violent or suicidal.

Some of the cultural factors that social scientists are studying for links to school conflict include whether exposure to violence on television and in the movies makes young people behave more aggressively and feel less empathy for others. What about playing video games that display vicious behavior or listening to song lyrics that glorify death and destruction? Does the ease of acquiring a gun affect students' attitudes toward problem solving and conflict resolution? If there is a link between violence in popular culture and school conflict, what should our society do about it?

Social scientists have tried to sort out society's role in school conflict by comparing the experiences of students in different cultures. They have also conducted many studies of American students to try to separate the importance of different social factors in the way students respond to stress and conflict. The results of these studies often conflict because the issue is complex and the data may be open to several different interpretations. Experts generally agree, however, that attitudes toward conflict resolution in our society influence attitudes toward conflict at school.

Violence in the Media

Ever since broadcast television became available in the late 1940s, social scientists have expressed concern about its influence on young people. Repeated polls have found that a majority of Americans believes television violence is harmful.

The wave of school shootings that occurred in the late 1990s re-energized the debate about connections between violent imagery in entertainment and violent acts by young people. Even news reports came under scrutiny for fear that publicity about school shootings would encourage copycat crimes.

Ever since broadcast television became available in the late 1940s, social scientists have expressed concern about its influence on young people.

Violent imagery is common in the media. One study looked at violent acts in prime-time television series, made-for-television movies, and music videos during the 1998–99 television season. It also examined fifty major movies released in theaters in 1998. The study found that:

- nearly all violent acts were shown on screen (for example, a knife fight), as opposed to showing only the effects of the violence (an ambulance removing an injured person)
- serious violence was shown as causing injuries or death less than half the time
- rarely was violence shown to cause emotional harm to anyone—the perpetrator, the victim, or witnesses
- good guys instigated violence almost as often as bad guys

- the majority of violent acts were concentrated in a small number of movies, television shows, and music videos
- on average, across all types of entertainment studied, one violent act occurred every two minutes

How Much Violence Do We See?

The American Psychological Association estimates that the average twelve year old has seen eight thousand murders and one hundred thousand acts of violence on network television alone.

Violent video and computer games have also come under scrutiny. Eric Harris, one of the shooters in the rampage at Columbine High School, played a customized version of the computer game *Doom*, which some believe was an electronic rehearsal for the school shooting. Other school shooters had spent long hours playing aggressive games such as *Quake* and *Redneck Rampage*. In these games, the player has a first-person perspective on violent, gory worlds where the choice is to kill as often as possible or be killed.

According to studies by Dr. Jeanne Funk, a child psychiatrist at the University of North Carolina, kids like violent and high-stress video games. If allowed, many kids will spend large amounts of time playing them. Do hours spent playing violent electronic games and watching violent media images change behavior? Many experts believe that it does. They think that reality and fantasy become blurred when violence is presented as entertainment and, as a result, people who see a lot of violent entertainment become less sensitive to the pain and suffering of others.

While studies have shown that children who see a lot of media violence are more aggressive, more likely to use force to solve problems, and more fearful of the world around them, not all experts accept the results of these studies. According to Colin Hatcher, chief executive officer of SafetyEd International, a nonprofit organization promoting the safe use of electronic technology by children and teens, "Some video games appear to be a bad influence on children while others are not. Scientific opinions are fairly divided on this issue. Some kids play violent games and become violent. Other kids play violent games and don't become more aggressive."

What experts do agree on is that violent teens watch more violent movies and play more violent video games than nonviolent teens. However, it remains unclear whether these experiences cause some teens to become violent or whether teens who already have violent tendencies simply seek out images and activities that reinforce their attraction to violence.

Guns and Society

Many Americans own guns. About four in every ten American homes have at least one gun. With so many guns in private hands, it is not surprising that some guns end up on school campuses. About 84 percent of the violent deaths at school are from gunshot wounds.

Michael Carneal, who killed three people at Heath High School in West Paducah, Kentucky, on December 1, 1997, used a pistol stolen from his neighbor's garage. Andrew Golden and Mitchell Johnson killed five people at Westside Middle School in Jonesboro, Arkansas, on March 24, 1998, using seven guns taken from Andrew's grandfather and three taken from his father. Of the guns Eric Harris and Dylan Klebold used at Columbine High School in Littleton, Colorado, one was bought for them by an eighteen-year-old

Weapons at School

In 1997, 13 percent of high-school boys and 4 percent of high-school girls said that they had brought a knife, a gun, or a weapon such as a baseball bat to school within the past month. Six out of every ten middle-school and high-school students said that they knew someone who could bring a gun to school if he or she wanted to. One-quarter of these students claimed that they personally could easily acquire a gun.

friend from an unlicensed seller at a gun show. The other was sold to them by an adult who knew that they were legally underage for owning an assault pistol.

Why is it so easy for students to get guns? One reason is simply because there are a lot of guns around. Another is the common practice of keeping firearms unlocked and loaded at home. More than half of all handguns are stored this way. Even in homes where children live, about one in ten families with guns keep them unlocked and loaded. Fewer than half keep their guns in the safest manner: with the guns locked away separately from the ammunition. Despite the fact that guns are used more often in suicides than in homicides and that for every justifiable homicide (for example, self-defense) there are 139 other gun deaths (suicides, murders, and accidental shootings), many people still insist that a loaded gun in the home is their best protection against criminals. Unfortunately, some of these guns are accessible to disturbed teens who take them to school.

Gun ownership is not the only reason why lethal violence erupts at school. In Switzerland and Israel, almost every adult man has a gun, and military service is mandatory. However, in these countries, gun violence—both in society and in schools—is much lower than it is in the United States. Other countries such as Canada, Great Britain, Germany, and Japan have strict laws limiting gun ownership. Although these countries have much less gun violence than the United States, school shootings still occur and teen suicide is a serious problem.

How Easy Is It for a Kid to Get a Loaded Gun?

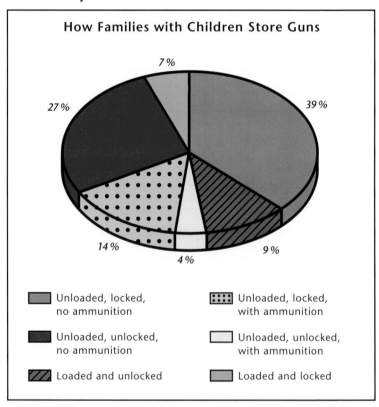

How Families with Children Store Guns

7%
27%
39%
14%
4%
9%

- Unloaded, locked, no ammunition
- Unloaded, locked, with ammunition
- Unloaded, unlocked, no ammunition
- Unloaded, unlocked, with ammunition
- Loaded and unlocked
- Loaded and locked

Fewer than 40 percent of families who have children living at home stored their guns in the most secure manner: with the guns unloaded, locked, and kept separate from the ammunition. (Source: The National Center for Health Statistics, 1999.)

Even strict gun-control laws did not prevent Robert Steinhaeuser, a nineteen year old who had been expelled from his school in Erfurt, Germany, from returning to the school on April 26, 2002, with a handgun and a shotgun and killing sixteen people before committing suicide. Robert was a member of two gun clubs and had met all of Germany's strict requirements for legal gun ownership. This was the worst school shooting in Europe since March 13, 1996, when seventeen people were killed in a shooting at Dunblane Primary School in Scotland, another country with strict gun laws.

The framers of the Bill of Rights recognized the right of private citizens to own guns, addressed in the Second Amendment to the Constitution of the United States. Because of the value put on private gun ownership, the United States has been much slower to enact gun-control legislation than Canada, Japan, and most European countries. In the United States, the attitudes of the public and of politicians toward guns and the issue of gun control are complex and emotional. The current combination of the availability of guns and the images that teens see in the media of characters using guns to solve their conflicts makes it hardly surprising that some students turn to guns to solve their problems at school.

Five

Preventing
School Violence

n Port Huron, Michigan, a quiet town of forty thousand about 60 miles (95 kilometers) northeast of Detroit, Justin Schnepp and Jedaiah Zinzo, two fourteen-year-old boys, were up to something. Daniel Fick and Jonathan McDonald seemed to be in on the plans, too. In May 1999, a few weeks after the shooting at Columbine High School in Littleton, Colorado, several classmates at Holland Woods Middle School overheard the four boys talking about how they were going to do a "Colorado repeat."

Dana Thomas, Justin's twelve-year-old girlfriend, heard Justin and Jon talking about going to school and shooting people, but she didn't think they were serious. Vanessa Fuller heard Justin talking to Dan about smuggling guns from his grandfather's house into the school, taking over the office, calling an assembly, then massacring the student body so that they could kill more people than Dylan Klebold and Eric Harris had at Columbine.

The next day, Vanessa told the principal what she had heard. The principal called the police who interviewed the boys and then arrested them. They were charged with conspiracy to commit murder. Another student came forward and said that he had been asked by one of the boys to draw a map of the school. A short time later, a bomb was found near the school, although it was never linked to the four boys. Assistant School Superintendent Thomas Miller called Vanessa a hero for telling the principal about the threats she had overheard.

In the courts, the case against Jonathan was dismissed. Daniel, age 13, was tried as an adult on the charge of conspiracy to commit first-degree murder; he was found not guilty. Justin and Jedaiah pleaded guilty to lesser charges. No one at Holland Woods Middle School was injured.

Before the 1990s, many people believed school violence and weapons on campus were problems only in poor, inner-city schools. The school shootings that started in the 1990s showed this was not true. Shooting after shooting happened at predominantly white, middle-class schools in small towns or suburban areas. Parents and students began realizing that school shootings were only the most extreme form of school

Shooting after shooting happened at predominantly white, middle-class schools in small towns or suburban areas.

conflict. Even in wealthy suburban schools, bullying and harassment went on every day. Parents, school officials, and students started asking, "How can we make our schools safe?"

Zero Tolerance

Starting around 1990, school officials responded to the increased threat of school violence by enforcing a zero-tolerance policy for weapons, drugs, fighting, aggressive behavior, and sexual harassment on school property. Zero-tolerance policies require predetermined punishments for *any* violation of a rule. It does not matter whether the violation is meant as a serious threat or as a joke. Punishment is usually automatic suspension or expulsion.

Between 80 and 90 percent of schools in the United States have zero-tolerance policies. Zero tolerance is intended to make schools safe by:

- letting students know the school is serious about enforcing the rules

- removing a threat the first time it happens
- enforcing uniform punishment regardless of the age, gender, race, social status, or reputation of the person making the threat

In 1994, passage of the federal Gun-Free Schools Act reinforced the policy of zero tolerance. For any student who takes a gun to school, this law requires that the student be expelled from school for one year and referred to the juvenile justice system.

People agree that schools need to be safe, but not everyone agrees that zero-tolerance policies are the right way to make them secure. Some principals claim that zero-tolerance rules are written so broadly and are so inflexible that principals are forced to punish students who violate rules in seemingly harmless ways.

In October 1996, a sixth grader in Columbia, South Carolina, brought a steak knife to school with her lunch. When she asked a teacher for permission to use it at lunchtime, school officials called the police and quickly suspended her. A similar incident occurred in Alexandria, Louisiana, in February 1997, when a second grader was suspended for bringing a pocket watch for show and tell that had a one-inch knife attached to it. In Jonesboro, Arkansas, a town that had had a school shooting in 1998, a first grader was suspended in 2001 for picking up a breaded chicken finger at lunch, pointing it at a teacher, and making gun noises.

When Rights Collide

Sometimes it is difficult for schools to balance the civil rights of an individual student with the rights of his class-mates to a weapon-free school environment. Gurbaj Singh was a twelve-year-old boy who lived in a suburb of Montreal, Canada. While playing basketball at school one day, a four-inch dagger he wore under his clothes fell to the ground. Gurbaj is a Sikh. Sikhism is a religion founded about five hundred years ago in northern India. Like all baptized Sikh men, Gurbaj wears a small dagger called a *kirpan* under his clothes. To Sikhs, the kirpan is a religious symbol, not a weapon. It is worn to remind them of the presence of God. Wearing one is a religious obligation.

Since the age of five, Gurbaj had never removed his kirpan, not even to sleep. When the school principal, in keeping with a zero-tolerance policy for weapons, de-manded that Gurbaj hand over the dagger, Gurbaj chose to walk home rather than obey the principal and break his religious vow. This put him at the center of a court case. On one side, Quebec Minister of Justice Paul Begin said, "The maintenance of security in schools requires zero tolerance for the carrying of knives." And some parents at Gurbaj's school agreed. One father asked, "With all the violence that appears in schools these days, why allow a weapon in school?"

But Gurbaj did not budge. "I cannot part with my kirpan because it is part of the obligation I accepted when I took my baptism," he said. A lower court ruled that Gurbaj could return to school if his kirpan remained securely fastened in a wooden sheath and was worn beneath his clothes. But the school rejected this ruling. In 2002, the case was headed to the Supreme Court of Canada.

Peer Mediation

Name-calling, gossiping, someone flirting with your girlfriend or making fun of your clothes in front of your friends—these things happen every day in school. But somehow it seems that a lot of adults don't understand how infuriating and upsetting social insults can be. Yet most fights at school begin with things that adults would consider minor social matters.

Peer mediation is a way for students to help other students resolve conflicts that might otherwise escalate toward violence. Students who choose to become peer mediators get special training to help their classmates settle everyday disputes. No one is forced to take a conflict to a peer mediator, but many students choose to because they feel someone their own age will understand the situation better than an adult.

Heather Kwartz was a peer mediator at Kennedy High School in Fremont, California. She was trained in a daily peer-resource class for which she received high-school credit. "We were trained in activities like active listening, asking open-ended questions, and team building. We also learned how to guide a person to a decision through questioning and not giving advice, and in understanding verbal and nonverbal communication," she says. Heather and her fellow peer mediators also received conflict-resolution training. Conflict resolution helps people involved in a disagreement to come to an understanding that is acceptable to both of them. "We mediated conflicts between friends who had temporarily become rivals and between students who had problems with each other and had been enemies for a long time."

The role of peer mediators is not to take sides or to decide who is right or wrong. Instead, they listen and help work out solutions that seem fair to both parties. The information they get during a mediation session is kept confidential—no gossiping to friends or adults about other people's problems. The only exception is when a peer mediator receives information that a life may be at stake—for example, if someone says they are thinking about suicide. No student is forced to use the peer mediator or accept the mediator's solution, but many students who

The role of peer mediators is not to take sides or to decide who is right or wrong. Instead, they listen and help work out solutions that seem fair to both parties.

have tried the process find that it works. Other students understand the importance of social concerns that adults might brush off as unimportant "kids' stuff."

Heather believes that a lot of conflict at school arises from the images people try to present to the world. "People are trying to find where they fit in. A lot of conflict starts when someone says something that knocks down an image someone else wants to project. Then they feel they have to protect that image." Her advice on avoiding school conflict is that communication is key. "People have to learn not just to express their feelings but also to listen actively to what others are saying."

Personal Responsibility

Schools are looking for ways to help angry, alienated students become more connected to their teachers and to their community. Peer mediation, along with anger-management and negotiation-skills programs all help make schools less violent places. Unfortunately, many schools lack the time, money, and staff to run programs like these. Sometimes churches and other organizations in the community make these programs available. But ultimately, every person in the school community has to take personal responsibility for making his or her school a safe and violence-free place.

As a student, the most important thing you can do is tell a responsible adult if you believe someone has a weapon or is planning a violent act. Unfortunately, many students think that telling is the same as "tattling" and are reluctant to speak up when they have seen someone with a weapon or have overheard plans involving violence. In one study, only about half the students in grades seven through twelve said that they would tell an adult if they overheard someone planning a school shooting.

Speaking up about a threat is the best way to stop the violence. Passing this information along to a responsible adult is not the same as tattling. It may even keep the people planning the violence from spending the rest of their lives in jail. More than three-quarters of school shooters told others, sometimes repeatedly, about their plans before they acted.

You can help create a violence-free environment in your school by practicing tolerance in your social life. Be a

Managing Anger

Anger is most often a response to feelings of embarrassment, humiliation, or frustration. Everyone gets angry occasionally, but learning to control an angry response is an important step toward becoming an adult. Here are a few things you can do the next time you feel angry:

- Take a few deep breaths and concentrate on relaxing. Silently count to ten, sing a song or say a prayer in your head, or do anything else that gives you time to relax.

- Think before you act. You do not have to respond right away or even respond at all. It often takes a stronger person to walk away from a situation than to stay and fight.

- Remind yourself that you are your own boss and that you are not going to let someone else control you by tempting you into losing your temper.

- Practice mouth control. Say nothing until you can say it calmly, or use silence as your weapon.
- Pretend that what has been said to you does not bother you. If you do not respond, your tormentor is likely to stop bothering you, and the fact that you are secure enough to be unconcerned raises your standing among your friends.
- Do not argue in front of friends where you may feel pressured to defend your honor or where an argument can spread to involve other people.
- Stay out of other people's disagreements. Walk away from other people's fights. In many arguments, an audience only adds fuel to the fire.
- Once you have calmed down, try to figure out what makes you angry. Is it being called stupid or weak? Is it having someone you care about put down or disrespected? Everyone has anger triggers. Knowing yours helps you stay in control.

good friend, quick to listen to others and slow to judge them because they are different from you. If a friend sounds depressed or troubled, encourage him or her to get help from a counselor or trusted teacher. Take seriously all threats of suicide and talk about death. Some people falsely believe that talking about suicide encourages someone to act. People who talk about wanting to die already

Speaking up about a threat is the best way to stop the violence.

have the idea of suicide in their minds. Encourage them to talk to a counselor or another responsible adult or to call a suicide hotline.

Drugs and alcohol decrease self-control and cloud a person's judgment. Under their influence, simple arguments can quickly become violent. Discourage retaliation for wrongs you feel have been done to you or your friends. Learn to give someone room to walk away from an argument with dignity.

Teasing, gossiping, and name-calling can hurt. Ask adults you know, and you will find that they vividly remember some painful put-downs from their school years. No one likes every person at school, but disliking someone is no excuse for teasing or bullying them. Respect is not earned by building yourself up through belittling or tearing down someone else. Your behavior can make your school a less stressful place to spend your days.

"There is so much pain on both sides of the bully/bullied relationship and it lasts a long time, but it does not have to last forever," says Heather McCutcheon. "I am a mother now, and my goal is to raise my son to know his own worth and recognize the worth of others." Remember—you don't have to blow out someone else's candle to make your own burn brighter.

Glossary

bullying: repeated intimidation or aggression by a person with more power toward a person with less power

corporal punishment: hitting, beating, striking, spanking, or otherwise using physical force to punish a person

depression: a condition of long-lasting negative thoughts and sadness; a person experiencing depression loses interest in normally pleasurable activities, may withdraw from friends and family, and may have changes in eating and sleeping patterns

dysfunctional family: a family that is unable to cope with the stresses of daily life; members of dysfunctional families may have substance-abuse problems, legal problems, severe financial problems, and/or mental-health disorders

extortion: making someone turn over something of value by using force or threats

felony: a serious crime; people who have committed felonies are usually restricted from owning guns

firearm: any handgun, rifle, shotgun, or assault weapon

handgun: a revolver or pistol that is designed to be fired with one hand; handguns are generally small firearms that are easy to conceal

harassment: a pattern of taunts, name-calling, and low-level conflict repeatedly aimed at the same person

hate words: hostile and offensive words that are used against people because of their race, ethnic background, religion, gender, sexual orientation, or disability

homicide: murder

mayhem: intentional damage, crippling, or disfigurement of any part of the body school violence: any physical attack or threat of attack with or without weapons that occurs on school property or at school-sponsored events

sexual harassment: unwanted and inappropriate comments about another person's body, sexual activity, or sexual preferences; or inappropriate touching, pinching, or caressing of someone who does not want that type of attention

suicide: the intentional taking of one's own life

zero-tolerance policy: a policy in which every violation of a rule is treated with the same punishment, and there is no room to make adjustments based on the circumstances surrounding the violation

Further Resources

Books

Izenberg, Neil, and Steven Dowshen eds. *Human Diseases and Conditions. Supplement I, Behavioral Health.* New York: Charles Scribner's Sons, 2001.
A secondary-school encyclopedia covering emotional-health concerns such as depression, bullying, peer pressure, and school avoidance.

Menhard, Francha Roffe. *School Violence: Deadly Lessons.* Berkeley Heights: Enslow Publishers, 2000.
Another view of school violence.

Sadler, A.E., ed. *What Causes Juvenile Crime and Violence: Opposing Viewpoints.* San Diego: Greenhaven Press, 1997.
Thought-provoking essays taking opposite points of view about the causes of youth violence.

Sanders, Pete, Steve Myers, and Mike Lacey. *Bullying (What Do You Know about).* Brookfield: Copper Beach Books, 1996.
Problems caused by bullies and how to cope with them.

Periodicals

Bower, Amanda. "Scorecard of Hatred." *Time*, 19 March 2001, 30+.
A summary of foiled and executed school violence since the shooting at Columbine High School.

Greenberg, David. "Students Have Always Been Violent: They're Just Better Armed Today." *Slate*, 7 May 1999.
A history of school violence that puts current concerns into historical perspective.

Kowalski, Kathiann. "What Teens Are Doing about Violence." *Current Health 2* 27(7) (March 2001): 6–12.
Stories about students developing programs to prevent school violence.

Orr, Tamra B. "Students Keeping the Peace." *Current Health 2* 28, no.4 (December 2001): 28–30.
Story of how David Winkler, a high-school student, started the Pledge Against School Violence.

Rinaldo, Denise. "What's a Bully?" *Scholastic Choices* 17, no.2 (October 2001): 12.
A discussion of bullying and how students can resolve problems with bullies.

"The Columbine Tapes." *Time*, 20 December 1999, 40+.
One of the most readable recountings of the shootings at
Columbine High School.

Organizations

American Psychological Association
Office of Public Affairs
750 First St., NE,
Washington, DC 20002
(800) 374-2721
www.apa.org
This organization of professional psychologists offers information for the public on social and emotional health
problems through their website or by mail.

Committee for Children
568 First Ave. South, Ste. 600
Seattle, WA 98104
(800) 634-4449
www.cfchildren.org
Provides information on social skills and training programs
for educators and families.

National Center for Conflict Resolution Education

Conflict Resolution Education Inc.

P.O. Box 17241

Urbana, IL 61803

(217) 384-4118

www.resolutioneducation.com

Information on conflict resolution and training.

National School Safety Center

141 Duesenberg Dr., Ste. 11

Westlake Village, CA 91362

(805) 373-9977

www.nssc1.org

Information on creating safe schools.

Online sites

American Academy of Child & Adolescent Psychiatry, Facts
for Families, #37: Children and Firearms,
www.aacap.org/publications/factsfam/firearms.htm
Information sheets on social and emotional health issues such
as children and firearms, children's threats, and depression.

American Psychological Association Help Center, Warning Signs, www.helping.apa.org/warningsigns
Developed in conjunction with MTV, this site explains the warning signs of school violence, how to handle anger, what students can do to prevent school violence, and where to get help.

Center for Media and Public Affairs, www.cmpa.com
Extensive analysis of violence in television, movies, and music videos. Easily understood summary statistics are available in the Quick Facts listing.

Center for the Prevention of School Violence, www.ncsu.edu/cpsv
A selection of recent research findings about school violence, with links to the original research.

ERIC Clearinghouse on Counseling and Student Services, Bullying in Schools, ericcass.uncg.edu
An excellent website with a variety of information on bullying written for elementary and secondary students, parents, teachers, and mental-health professionals.

National Crime Prevention Council, www.ncpc.org
Information on what students, teachers, and communities can do to prevent school violence by the organization that runs the McGruff "Take a Bite Out of Crime" Program.

www.bullying.org
A site where children from around the world can share their stories about being bullied and can respond to the stories of others.

Other Sources

Fight for Your Rights: Take a Stand Against Violence. Office of Juvenile Justice and Delinquency Prevention, 1999. Developed in conjunction with MTV, this CD-ROM features musicians and interactive scenarios for students on violence-related issues. Available free at ojjdp.ncjrs.org

Mediation: An Alternative That Works.
A video for middle-school students showing the peer-counseling process. Available from School Mediation Associates, 134 W. Standish Rd., Watertown, MA 02472; (617) 926-5969; www.schoolmediation.com

Index

About the Author

Tish Davidson graduated from the College of William and Mary and from Dartmouth College with degrees in biology. For many years, she has written about medical topics. She especially enjoys making complex information understandable to people without medical or scientific backgrounds. Tish lives in Fremont, California.

Thanks to my editors Meredith DeSousa and Nikki Bruno at Scholastic Library Publishing.